A Poet's Secrets

Anoucheka Gangabissoon

Scarlet Leaf

2017

ISBN   978-1-988827-25-4

PUBLISHED BY SCARLET LEAF

Toronto, Canada

ISBN   978-1-988827-25-4

PUBLISHED BY SCARLET LEAF

Toronto, Canada

This collection of poems is dedicated to Life

And to everything that makes it up!

ACKNOWLEDGEMENT

1. I wish to thank my family for having made me who I am.

2. I wish to thank all my teachers and tutors who shaped me and my love for writing.

3. I wish to thank my preface writer and my afterword writer.

4. I wish to thank all my readers for their appreciation and support.

INTRODUCTION

A Poet's Secrets is my third collection of poems. Poems which I have been writing since the year 2013. Should you require from me, answers, as to why and how I write, I should tell you then, that writing is for me, a most enjoyable process. To write lines and lines of poems which may be interpreted by each and every one, as they would deem it best and to leave them here, forever, is a dream come true. Of course, I write impulsively, I write, as if driven, having as aim, the pouring out of my inner accumulated magmatic swells.

As the title indicates, the poetic manifestations included in this collection are my most precious secrets. They are that which I would never ever talk about, with anyone. Yet, here I am, brought to sharing them with the whole world, as poems presented in this collection.

I hope you will enjoy reading them. I hope you will be able to identify yourself with that which I have written, on the personal and emotional planes as well as that of the mysterious yet hard to define attributes of faith.

Together, let's celebrate of the enigma that makes poets who they are!

Anoucheka Gangabissoon

PREFACE

Anoucheka is a compulsive writer with a raging passion for poetry – a zest which ripples across all the lines she pens intensely. In A Poet's Secrets, she shares her love for nature, a source of joy, inspiration and solace. She feels intimately connected with the elements and the beauty of the sun, moon and stars never cease to make her wonder at the grand cosmic plan they meticulously exhibit. Spirituality oozes out of the soulful simplicity of words with a warm rhythm echoing the urge to explore the mysticism pf existence. Simply and deeply, perennial existential concerns of life, death and relationships are probed, insights are shared and answers are sought gropingly. Yet, the poet's faith in God transcends all skepticism caused by bitter experiences. She rises, awakened by spiritual vigor and strengthened by the catharsis of feelings. Love, a common theme in Anoucheka's verse, has a fresh directness spanning the extremes of despair and bliss as well as the shades between. The poet revels in the creative power of self-expression, a ritual with quasi-religious undertones.

Creativity lives not only for the Creator
As beings with morals, we do have a hand in this matter!

The Damned

9

Anoucheka affirms the sanctity of the poet as a creator with a moral choice in a world drifting away from values. Her young questing voice must be heard.

Suniti Nundoo-Goorah
Senior Lecturer
Open University of Mauritius

1. THE HOLY AMEN

Long live the holy amen
A real solace for all men
It protects and gives refuge
A little word with a meaning so huge!

A real distress lies for those who have at hand
The evil doer at a close stand
Yet, to vanquish all with its magic wand
Does this little word do when uttered as amen!

Spoken of in the religious books
A sharp weapon bringing down the crooks
A word meant for those with faith
Whether uttered with the heart or with the
breath

Used when mercy is shown
Coming from the skies, windblown
Showered with pitiful tenderness
As a way to cure the swollen abscess!

Long live the holy amen

Celebrated in the world of man

So beautiful it is, like the garden of Eden

Yes, indeed long live the holy amen!

2. NIGHT FANTASIES

The night is when I shed off my worldly attire

The night is when I am myself

A being of mystery

A being having a celestial lover

A being so enamoured

That the magnificence of my love

Can have no match and no rival!

The night is when I dive into the pool of my sub-
consciousness

The night is when my passionate thirst is
quenched

Then when I travel to the skies

And bid my heart to skip a few more beats!

Why, the night is when I become a goddess

A most beautiful one

With a glow of fire pulsating in my heart

Yes, the night is when I travel to the other realms

To bid my muse,

A being of passion as well

To be patient

I shall come to him

Of course, I shall

I am just trapped in this world of endless cycles

I am just trapped in between the reactions of my
actions

But I shall come

Have faith!

And there, while the night lasts on Earth

There, we drown in each other's engulfing love

There, in that place

Illuminated by a thousand moons

There, where stars can be plucked

There, where the night can be as long as we want
it to be

Why, the night time

The time for me to be who I really am

The time for my amorous suffering to end

The time, the time

To be captured in this most glorious verse!

3. THE GREAT MAN

A great man walked by

He had no suit, no tie

Yet he made the world sing a lullaby

A song to be remembered by all those who

walked by

A man with no other

He easily made me falter

For I kept him since then in my soul

And yearn only for his call

A wish known to none

To my own destiny I am prone

Relying on my own lucky stone

I envy his mystical bone

Glory be to his footsteps

Those which made the whole world rock

That one voice grown on mishaps

Oh how easily would I wear his frock

Pray Lord, hear my song

My life's length, either short or long

May be put to good use

For such a cause, with you I would play a game

of truce!

4. THE PAST PRESENT AND FUTURE

Broken is my present
Broken with my own torment
It can only to be in lament
While I seek not any fruity fulfillment

Flourishing is my past
Though it could not last
I brewed spells to cast
On my own preys, so varied and vast!

Insecure is my future
I see it not as an adventure
Rather, it is for me a torture
One made out by the Gods, with great measure

As for my own self
It pities its material self

Wishing to be as free as an elf
It seeks solace in the eternal self

What of my own moan
Though I buried it deep in the lawn
It remains in my soul, as if sewn
Sewn to my love, to my own lost throne!

5. THE GAME OF LOVE

Love happens with no measure
Nor it is an adventure
Nor is it a piece of pricy furniture
Rather, it is to be taken as a great leisure

A walk in a flowery garden
A dance in the courts of Eden
A swing in the mysticism of Amen
A leisure, as comforting as our own brethren

Hey Cupid, why do you act with zeal
When love you can't even conceal
When you can't even hear my appeal
When you decide on the rules of the deal

Love ends with no measure
Someday it turns out to be a stricture
It becomes so easily a game of defeature
At worst, it turns into a caricature

Then it becomes a game of the strongest

The winner is the one who runs furthest

The one who can cry less

And he turns thus, to be simply senseless!

6. MY SEARCH

Should I find that which I seek
Should I find it if I remain mild and meek
Though I tend not to be a freak
I crumble many times for I become weak

Weak when faced with adversity
Weak when faced with the enemy
Weak for I lose all my credibility
That which could take me to the land of eternity

Long was the hour
Living it, I lost my power
Savoring it, I dived in blunder
And forsaking it made me an abhorrer

Great was the length of my mind
Though it chose not to remain blind
It became my own mace

To be lost in it became my sole solace

Maybe in it shall I find that which I seek
Even if I keep not myself as meek
I shall always search in those creeks
Down where I am the Queen of all mystics!

7. PRAY

Pray to the Lord of the skies
With Him, we shall all rise
Reaching up to a high pedestal
Rising up to his abode, so magical

Pray to have His gaze showered on you
He shall rid you of your mood so blue
And keep you in a blissful hue
For you thought of him as being true

What He gives, I accept
What He breathes, I respect
For He is none other than my maker
The one to rule my cosmos, for now and ever!

Like me, relish His alms
Drown in his hidden charms
Love the toils He bestows
They shall be gone with the wind's flows!

Pray to the Lord of the skies

He shall keep you by His side

Whether it be lame or wise

He shall keep you safe in his stride!

8. MY TREASURED GEM

My soul treasures only one gem
That is the eternal stem
Emanating from the mystic river
Into which love flows forever

Whatever be His name
Whatever He be known as
He is the one and same
The one to fill us with joy and love

Knowing not what He seems
Having seen Him only in my dreams
I let my vision run free
Hoping for a bout of His mercy

Come, come and rid me of my hurdles
True, with them, life seems not so pleasurable
For I suffer the sins of my actions
And resort, for solace, to their reactions!

My soul suffers only for the one gem

Known as the One to give the final word

He brings forth

Life and death!

My sole treasure

I shall see Him at the time of my worldly

departure

His abode awaits

My soul, meanwhile, frets!

9. LOVE AND ITS END

At one time, I knew the essence of love
I was then, a frail and free dove
Yet, angered must have been the One above
For he filled me with pain and disdain

Came to my face, hot tears
Laughed at was I by my peers
Still, I chose not to change steers
Rather, my love grew even in arrears

Pining, I breathed
Hurting, my heart heaved
Dreams I weaved
In the end, my soul was aggrieved!

Broken and shattered
Torn and destroyed
I was now coerced

Life with faith was to be a ploy

Love was set aside
My being became my pride
Solo was I to enjoy life's ride
And avenues did open up to my stride!

10. FOR MY LORD

For my Lord, I shall forsake Life
Whatever may be the state of my breath
Whether it be filled with greatness
Or it be filled with blankness

To my Lord I shall abide
For He is the one who makes my ride
And fills me with utmost pride
Even if he chooses to remain subtle and unseen!

For His sight am I keen
For His grace I would be a Queen
For His word I would give up all I own
Even if it be a diadem or a mighty throne!

Cruel though He may be
Giving me my dues with sincerity
He remains my sole master
My one great savior!

Desirable though He may be

When pleased he is in my mystery

Yet, I remain always thirsty

For the time of my great revelation!

A Lord still unknown

Still feared and still remembered

I shall keep myself to his whims, to it I am

always prone

Till He chooses to have my thirst quenched!

11. MY BOON

It came as a boon
A boon much awaited, much prayed for

Shining through the darkness
It illuminated my soul, lost in distress

A new way opened up to me
Now I could see eternity

Lying beyond my blinded vision
It was there, all the time, lost in its own
attraction

O Death, I await your grace
When I shall see you face to face

Then only shall I know love
Known as the solace of the One Above

Thirsty, I wait

Hurry, call I to fate

A boon with an aim

That of keeping me not in maim!

To my Lord I shout hence

Pray, give me another glimpse of your dance!

12. THE WAYS OF LIFE

Whether it be cold or frozen

Whether it be warm and shiny

Life is nothing but a burden

A burden yet so temporary

Imbibed with the mystery of the Lord

It surely deserves an award

There where imperfections are concerned

For everywhere only the good is discerned

Known as stupidity

The short minded cares only for its reality

Known as gullibility

The foolish ones are meant to be lost in its

ambiguity

So whether it be night and day

To you I shall always say

Pray, be not mistaken
You shall carry your own burden

What you see is not the real
See behind the bluish veil
And revere my own zeal
It is in search of the no pareil!

13. MY DUTY

Once, when the day was cold and misty
I set out for a trip down to a lonely spot
Filled with gardens so flowery
There, I settled down and started a work of art

Yet, my poetry was all rotten and stale
Nothing could cure my stagnant mind
Not even a sip of ale
Harshly, I chose to leave my art behind

When O Magic, O Pure Bliss
An angel appeared, all pink and filled with peace
He took my pen in his hand
And gave me verses to tend

Beautiful, Lyrical
None could be more mystical
Before he left, on my cheeks, he left a kiss
And said, Fear never the evil adder's hiss!

Remember, the garden of Eden

Is still full of angels, so awakened

So relish in your poetry

As if it were your sole duty!

14. THE AIM OF LIFE

Thought I of my aim
Thought I of how life is lame
Sitting in front of my keys
Dreaming of being the Queen of words

I wonder at my own fate
Do we all have one?
Shall we ever be satiate?
If our Fate keeps on being as elusive as the
golden swan?

Maybe somewhere,
Someone, in his lair,
Does enjoy this show
And does ponder at our woe

Yet, we all belong to this place
Known to be of great solace
It keeps us happy in many ways

There, indeed, the physical knows not any
decays!

And what of love?
Surely nothing but an obsession
A need, to seek for attention
A need to seek liberation!

Freedom from this vicious circle
Freedom to see beyond the blue veil
Free shall I be someday
Meanwhile, let me ponder at how life can be
lame!

15. SUCH A STRONG LOVE

Mystical being, so dark and so deep
For you, the mountains are no more steep
Wise and witty, you easily become sweaty
When enamored you become by my temper so
misty

With a strong love so sincere
You destroy my whole sphere
Never again shall I be empty
For your love fills me entirely

Desirous to see my beauty
You shall even attempt every possibility
A gentle touch, warming up my hand
For you, I shall wait till the end

Faced with the strength of that love, Time shall
lose

Faced with the strength of that love, the skies

shall be let loose

Cupid shall never again be mean

And humankind, for our love, shall be keen!

16. THE HOLY CREATURE

At the beginning of Creation
There was never anything like abomination
Resisting the vices of the Evil God
Man lived peacefully in his house of mud

Then came the intoxication of sin
The good and meek were changed into filth
Whatever was left of the divine
Became known as Time left behind

Mystically, a Holy Creature appeared
Powerful, she was to be eternally revered
Her path was full of obstacles
Stoic, she fought alone and made miracles

On a quest, she had already embarked
Satan had her fate as already marked
A real beauty, she shall be winsome

Victory! When creation will realize she was
awesome!

17. THE ORACLE

Comfort we all seek from the Oracle

Guidance we all need from its parable

Reassurance we yearn for our existence

Powerful it is, for it calms our annoyance

Should we find some truth

From those sitting behind those booths

For we know not if protected shall be our states

As their words do guide us in our Fates

Solace we all seek from the absurd

Impatient we all are to hear the holy word

Even if forgotten we have of our Lord

So entangled we are in our own discord

Comfort we all seek from the Oracle

Humorous is such a spectacle

Yet we all need it as if it were a miracle

As if a prediction of tomorrow could be

believable!

Calming words of sooth, reflection of the

Herculean

Blind those wise fools with your own tools

Help them arise

For they no longer are wise!

18. ON THAT DARK NIGHT

The dark stormy night
Shone with hazy starlight
The cries of our love so smoky
Made even the whole world seem sexy

A sip of a wine so red
Made my heart and soul bleed
I felt all powerful
As if I was the only one with blessings in
bountiful

Mysterious is the world
Its fires are all so cruel
Yet, beautiful are its skies
When love is accompanied by our cries

Intoxicated with passion, I am now all colored

Lost in love, I am now all enamored

Lost in love, fallen in desire, I ask for a melody

A divine one, lasting for the whole of eternity!

19. THE NEW DECREE

The devil shall not dare to fight
Scared he is, at the sight of the white light

The murderous shall never offend
Numb, they can only bear with their own stand

The miserable shall never lament
Happy they are in their own torment

The diseased shall never be in pain
Stoic they are, even if they are in great disdain

The sinners shall never disobey
Repentance they shall seek in the abbey

The selfish shall forget their ego
They shall fight for other's sorrow

The immoral shall never again be heretical

Saintly, they shall read the holy verses of the
Cathedral

The inhuman shall never again be animalistic
Spiritual, they shall become altruistic!

This new decree was written on a page
As the moon settles on a new age

Spoke thus the Master of Creation
Sorrowful at the sight of abomination

20. FREEDOM

Forever now shall we be free

Never again shall we fear the enemy

Even if our soul is all scared

We shall show him our teeth, all bared

Indulging in our crazy memories

We could be seen as the rabid

Though we are called not the morbid

We shall always recount our past stories

Enjoy we our freedom

Crave we not the gates of a new kingdom

Left all alone to enjoy our grace

Pray, may we not fall again into disgrace!

Life is made of many a path

Why we do choose one or another

Is not meant for us to ponder

Yet, though it be difficult, let us enjoy a laugh

Forever now shall we be free, forever

Let us make a truce

We shall keep to the side of truth

For freedom is indeed nothing yet so cheaper!

21. ON A DARK ALLEY

On a dark alley, on that night, I got a fright
Alone and sad, I walked on and made an
encounter which pushed me into a trance
On that night, the cruel wind shook and the
harsh rain danced
While I got to learn of what is that power called
the dark light!

On that night, the one called Death to me, made
his essence known
He talked to me and showed me how, to his
proximity I was prone
As fragile as a pane of glass
Life does hold on only to itself, as if windblown
And remains for Death, his favorite time pass!

Death, a brooding figure all clad in black
With yellow eyes popping out of their sacks

Came in front of me, unclenched his teeth and
spoke thus
Dull may be this world of pain
So dull that it makes it easy for me to throw life
out of its lane!

Unaware of the fragility of their threads
Men and women dance on their own footsteps
Taking this temporality to be true
Believing not in the science of the Mighty One
Pretending to be as happy as the black swan!

Be warned, shouteth Death
Take caution and be no more frivolous
Let go of all that is pretentious
Seek solace in the Blessed Words, rather,
Those spoken by the seers, sons of the Holy
Father!

A creepy figure, all clad in black
Spoke thus to me with yellow eyes popping out of
their sacks
A queer message given by a queer image
A message to be easily discarded in this dark age
But on that dark alley, on that cold night, I begot
some enlightenment!

22. A DEAD MOUNTAIN

As dry as a dead mountain
Is the state of my heart, full of pain
Once it was a cheerful fountain
Yet, its joys got lost down memory lane!

Shall the events take a fateful turn?
Shall the Gods make the deep sea churn?
So that my dead mountain to life returns?
So that it be lush once more with the beautiful
cherries meant to be its earn?

A dead mountain, with my flowers withered
without my gardener's presence
All my days were spent in abstinence
Away from his love and caring enthrall
I become all dull and cold

Such a state

Would keep me wilted as at date

Maybe such is what is willed to me by Fate

As to suffer is my call, at a fast rate

Hope, says the good note

Hope remains for the fools to give it a vote

So let it be then should it be so

Else, I shall drown in my own woe!

23. A DREAM

A dream, difficult to harness
Abstract it is, difficult to be seen, like the Loch
Ness
With ambition, its ammunition is fired
Time is needed to attain it, Time which never
does get tired!

A dream, played on the keys of a piano
On those days, when the tide is low
Yet, with its current life does flow
Even if tears and pain remain in tow!

A dream, preceding a nightmare
One as hostile as the Bandit's lair
A dream, into which night knows not any end
As Evil does hold its whole floor at hand!

Such a dream is surely blurry

Never to be seen as illusory

Even if for now, the times are sulky

For the endings are seen as a remedy!

Yet, the awakening to realization

Remains full of promise

Dreams and reality face each other

I feel as if I do stand on the edge of a cliff!

24. A NEW DAWN

Shall the sun set
On this evening, marked by a duet
That of life's and mine own suffering hand
Faced with fate's fateful stand

Shall the new dawn rise to brighten
Even if stars shine to enlighten
Such can cause my love to awaken
Even if I keep it in my heart, all hidden

The coming of this new age
Brought out by the appearing of an image
That of a lost love, dead, but resuscitated
With time, it remains unabated

A new day, full of hope
We shall indeed learn to cope
With this cold air coming forth with a cold front

Even if Fate has kept for us, more than one rant

A new day, it keeps my eyes dancing
Filled with love and care for every being
A new day, at last, my heart is appeased
After ages, at last, the battle has ceased!

25. MY LONELY RIDE

Once I chose to set out on a lonely ride
All alone I managed to reach the steep
mountainside
Though, in the process, I nearly got swallowed by
the tide
And even nearly got drowned in the seas, so
wide!

Riding all alone on a golden saddle
I suddenly felt the air, with danger, begin to
rattle
Smoky and freaky, I felt all stinky
I was pricky and jumpy, and I felt shaken up
horribly

Yet, I held on fast, and my ride took me to
Absentia
It was a country as queer as the land of Narnia

There, lions did have wings
And humans did grow stings

There, I was made into a Queen
I ruled the land in its every field
From archery to philosophy
My duty was simply to rule in all honesty

After my journey did end
I had no more matters to attend
Forlorn I was when I was sent to exile
A once powerful Queen, I was now fallen in great
style!

Life is such a journey
Temporal and transient
Having a really strange intent
Indeed, its aims remain hidden in its own
philosophy!

26. A WAY TO ENTERTAIN

A sure way to entertain
It is, simply by going over the world of pain

Here, it is but a world of the mistaken
Those who can do nothing other than live with a
faith, shaken

Horrible is this way to entertain, it is indeed an
act of sin
Yet, it is surely the only way to win

Obviously the reason being the difficult times
The merry season does fluctuate with life's many
chimes

Sometimes we all become cold with hatred, at

other times we are warm with love

In all, we are simply like the tiny mouse,

pretending to be brave

Yet, it remains a sure way to entertain

This world of pain is since eons ago, tainted with

many a stain!

27. FOR THE SAVIOUR

Faced with your presence, I become like an
absence
Blind never to your peacock's dance
I just let myself fly in freedom's abundance
Forgetting that I was sheltered even if for me you
showed only abhorrence

Deep in life's mist, I got my existence's new gist
I would have to keep it clenched, my fist
I would need to learn to be both young and bold
Courageous even, for though free, I do still yearn
for your hold

In your presence, imbibed with your essence
I became a doomed flower
Frail and weak, pretending to be strong
Knowing that such can make me look so wrong

Today, I am still lost in a swirling maze

Pray, Life, let me see through that gaze

If love is not indeed a sinful disease

Why does it always keep me ill at ease?

Lost in the charm of your presence

I realize that life is but a timed out dance

Everything did already end

Even before it did already start

28. THE GREAT MEN OF ARTS

The Great Men of Arts
After pondering on the matter of the hearts
Took up the issue of work
What is the essence of work?
Was the big question

Is it a hurdle?
Is it made up of trouble?
Is it that which fills us with seizures
When it should work wonders
And fill us with many pleasures

After pondering, came the Great Men's
conclusion
Work is our sole mission
It is certainly not life's intermission
Neither is it a pain in remission
Nor it is an imposed obligation

Rather, it meant to be our passion
That which brightens our daily vision

To this decision of the Great Men, I do give my
approbation
Work is that which gives us prime satisfaction
Such was the decree, without any condition
Of the Great Men of Arts
On the issue of work!

29. THE EMPTY SHELL

An empty shell was on display
On solid grounds it did lay
It did put on a happy countenance
So much that jolly seemed its appearance

Little did know that it was an empty shell, with a
stone heart
It awoke only to the expectations of finding the
cart
That which rode to the land of the Nirvana
All alone, not driven by anyone, it did go as if it
was all fearless!

Its stone heart did crave for solace
It did lost that in disgrace
It hid this truth ferociously
So much that the whole world did see it as the
enemy

Its feelings were indeed as pure as snow
For it, and only for it, the magical winds did blow
Yet, it would keep on being an empty shell
Even if the rest of the world thought of it being
an object of hell!

30. THE SNAKE'S SOUL

The soul of a broken snake
Is never to be put at stake
It could bite with anguish
And do enjoy it with lots of relish

It does have a heart of gold
It does never get old
Even though it is called the snake's soul
Emotions do remain its main call

Such did I learn from a wise sage
A magician he was, worthy of being called a
mage
I did meet him when I was lost and sinking deep
into despair
A despair known to be as cruel as a whiff of
poisonous air

For one to have such a soul

For one to have such a heart

Is indeed a boon from that known as creation

Else what would it be, say, just what would it

be?

31. DEATH

Death, a much feared figure you are
To life itself, you do give bruises and many a scar
That of temporality
That of uncertainty

Death, the time is of poetic liberation
Free from bondage, free from your compulsion
A time seen as a moment of exaltation
Love, pain, sorrow, all have become mere
illusion!

My own death can never be repulsive
In that worldly realm, it is easy to deceive
Those lazy believers of age
Good or bad, their karma they do give in gage

Death, you do give the time when the soul is at

ease

You do allow the soul to be then carried by

fairies

Everything does become trivial and temporal

On your great moment, so painful!

Death, sayeth Donne, be not proud

Death, sayeth I, sound your bells loud

To Narcissus, you have been fake

But to me, you are the winner at stake!

32. STARRY NIGHT

Starry night, do hear my plight

Sad is my heart

My beloved has gone out of sight

And for my own part

I need to get a fresh start

At times, I turn into a bully

At other times, I become a mere cutey

As for most of the times, I just keep feeling sorry

I keep craving for his smile

Knowing that a glimpse of it shall keep me going

for only a little while

Lonely night in my lonely bed

Silly dreams do wash up in my head

Dreams of either his glance or of sharing with

him a dance

While being always with him, lost in good stance

Love, when true, is never done out of prudence!

Starry night, please do hear my plight
Light up the way to the Holy Lord
In deep trance, He hears not my word
Ready I am here, to give up my life for love
Even if am shaking and weeping like a lost dove

With grace, I shall fly
With delight, to Him, my heart I shall tie
Applauded we shall be, by the whole sky
I am sure, He does deserve to be My Beloved
So these words are for Him, to tell him of my
heart's whims!

33. GLORY AND THE AWAKENED

Glory shall not fall on the mistaken
Nor shall it strike the fallen
Nor shall it make of itself a burden
Rather, it shall be on the path of those awakened
Those who care not for this world, who see it as a
mere burden

Glory, a word meant not for all
Maybe it does go to the alms man
The one who sees only the Lord's call
The one, who with creation shall sing a duet
As he does watch the beauty of the sunset

Glory be to that which is in daily living
Glory be to that which is in sorry pining
Glory be to that which is so transient
For all that which is not so permanent
For all that shall be forgotten when they do get
downfallen

So would I say to the world, remain not as one of

the mistaken

Rise, rise in this world so glorious

Even if you are seen as one of the mad men

Care not, care not for this ill omen

Thunder and lightning shall then have you not

stricken!

34. LOVE

Love, what a beautiful word for those lucky
residents
Those who live in Eden and its many orients
Yet, nothing turns out to be more blatant
Than the sight of love as it does get lost down the
torrent

Indifference does come with abundance
Bees no longer do enjoy their dance
In fright, to the Almighty they do prance
In search for the lost love, lost with regrets in
adaman-ce

Eden, devoid of flowers and fragrance
A queen, fallen to the state of compliance
A king, fallen down in disturbance
So much that evil seems to be the mood of
creation!

Love, when shattered and broken

Does no more sound as a beautiful note

But when with hatred it is laden

It does become a state which one can never do

quote!

35. O SUN

O Seductive and Stunning sun
So lively and so joyful you are
Faced with your light, bandits do run
Lest your warmth does open up their sole scar!

My own world does bask in my own darkness
Except for my dreams in which I become not a
princess
Nor a poet, nor a pauper
But my own queen, having to tackle with my own
temper!

In love does lie my call to be submissive
In this world, I can hardly do breathe
Thankfully O sun you do warm up my life
Even if I remain, always, in my own dark and
moody world

O beauteous sun

Pray, do set my demons on a run

With life, I shall be renewed

For with grace, I have indeed been lured

Shine your warmth on this slave that I am

Do break the ice inside of my heart

My body becomes a mere corpse

Without your brightness, o seductive sun!

36. WHAT DREAMS ARE MADE OF

Dreams, my only escapisms
Not being any sorts of realisms or academisms
Dreams made only of altruisms and fairyisms
Dreams, there where my love lies engulfed in
mysticisms!

Dreams, made of the Lord's essence
I become there not a butterfly
But a moth craving for luminescence
Wild and free, as pig in a pigsty!

Dreams, the only place where I can let go
And speak of all that has never been said
All that pain in my veins which made of me one
with no tomorrow
All gets drained away, as it had been soothsaid!

Dreams, my own escapisms
To run away from reality
A harsh and cruel monstrosity
Made up of its own clarity!

Dreams, in you do allow me to surrender
Allow me to dive in you, deep down under
Be like a predator and do allow me to be your
own prey
Always do I wait, when will I be lost in your own
sway!

37. THE BOON OF LOVE

A boon was gifted to me at noon
At that time, the clock did strike with force
It was a time when into hiding went the moon
For the sun's ardor did make it coarse

A mystery it was, solved in a riddle
Unveiled it was to life, as a puzzle
Gone was to be the abominable
Remained only those who are so amiable

A boon, for the dreamy eyed
Love was her crime, in lengths, amplified
An escape she sought when she was crucified
Lest the darkness reigns over her soul, making
her feel damn!

Should love be a crime

Recidivism lies at its prime

A God given gift for the capricious

Hoping that such shall make her notorious!

38. SEARCHING FOR THE MAGICIAN

The day was long and the men strong
Nobody did sense that something was wrong
Men did march on, along the pavement
Feeling like their souls have been drowned in an
evil current

A heavy day it was, during which lime tasted not
sour
Rather, it did turn sweeter within the hour
The men moved uphill towards the silvery
crescent
They saw not that its halo was but magnificent

A journey it was, set out to find the magician
Once full of wisdom, he is now vagrant
For he loved and lost
And did regret at all cost!

The men were fixed on their intent
They had to find the magical crescent
They cared not for the lingering sun
And they did walk on all day without any fun

Unattainable, unreachable was the magician's
lair
Soon, the moon even seemed to be abominable
Winding and winding up we were up the lane
So much that we twisted up in creepy pain

The men did march on
They did turn sinister as the day wore on
No silvery crescent, no magician
Only misery, and it did make the journey so
lonely

When oh, oh blessings, from heaven
With a swift hand, from the skies the magician
did come
To all he did wave from the clouds
And all men chanted and danced

For though the magician be not found on Earth
He does take care of all that did take birth
From his abode up in the skies
Those sorry men he does scrutinize!

39. LOVING LIFE

Love seems to hang in the cool air
I feel like I am in the middle of nowhere
If God would see me, He would surely dance at
my sight
For I am sure, that creation does seem to have
been graced by my inner light

My beauty did attract life to my den
Little did I realize it then
Always is its essence sung in a romance
Always is it branded as would be the seekers of
its every science

I am sure the coming days are to be filled with
joy
No more shall I be taken as life's toy
Creativity does fill me up immensely
Say, shall I ever remain an object of curiosity?

Surely, plans do get hatched from Heaven
If not, why would I today feel like I am in a green
garden?

40. THE DAMNED

Damned shall be the lost ones
Basking in sin always as the guilty ones

Hoping to be always happy in materialism
Speaking of nothing but atheism

Misfits rather than spiritualists
They believe in life with its many twists

Dancing they are among the foolish moths
Attracted always to all the objects of sloths

Gone shall be the pure from this world
Gone, seeking another one, better than this one

Damned indeed shall remain those cursed
Damned till their savior shall shine from up
above

Ignorant fools, they bask in their own lies
Taking themselves to be the Gods of the skies

Creativity lives not only for the Creator
As beings with morals, we do have a hand in this
matter!

41. A BEES' TALE

Some dancing bees, to life, did stand up
They were angry, for stolen was their holy cup
Their Queen filled with sorrow
Tried her best to bring an end to this woe
She resigned from her seat and abandoned her
altar

A holy cup, much needed, much heeded
Of what use is now the bees' existence, they
seem blindfolded
Now that gone is their light, gone is their Queen
The dancing bees know not any more pleasure
Except that of searching for their cup with lots of
measure

News of the theft spread far and wide
Even to the God's realm, surely to Him the bees
would never lie
Horror! Shock! Bewilderment
Who could have dared to torment
Those peaceful bees, those who peacefully adorn
the sky!

Lo! Suddenly he did come, a powerful bird
He claimed to be the one who sneered
At the Holy Cup, so much that away it steered
In search of respect and freedom
Away to the land of the Lord!

When the Queen did hear the news
She wailed in genuine distress
She did renounce to secluded loneliness
Alone, in a foreign forest
She did cry over her cup, How could it have been
so reckless?

As for the dancing bees

They set themselves to work

No more shall they idle their time away in

dancing

Now, they shall try their best to please the Queen

Even if they are now without a most holy cup!

42. LOVE AND ME

Of what use is Love if absent is always the Lover?
Of what use are songs if deaf is to be the
listener?
Or if dumb is to be the singer?
Crave we not all to find our own landing?

Love, in such a state do I know thee
Love that is how our ties I do foresee
It is said that after the rainy clime does come the
sunshine
That the rain shall fade away and lag behind

The past, known as that which never does last
The present, thanks to which the future always
does start
Yet, life with arrows you do pierce
Those whom love did coerce!

What shall be the state of the beloved

Away always he is from the lover, even if he is

always applauded

What does happen to the lover

If the beloved does sink down under?

Of what use is wisdom away from freedom

The lover's gaze did take me up high

Some place found high up in the sky

There where love does fill up the whole kingdom!

43. DARK TIMES DO END

Longing turned into sorrow
There was to be no breakthrough
Longing turned into suffering
Misery finally rose up, bright and shining

Holy lights turned dark
None could ignite even a tiny spark
Faith turned into despair
As evil breathed everywhere

Happy days were foreseen
Patience could not remain keen
Happiness does linger in shadows
The boat of desire did shine in its own sorrows

Sad is the note of this verse
Its dawning was like a curse
Meant to be a mere missive
Its meaning is driven from an age long grief

Always was I an object of creation
Gifted was I with fire by the God of Passion
Nothing could deter my determination
Nothing, especially when success did follow and
brought me to elation!

44. LIFE'S BLESSINGS

A blessing is hidden in your bruise

Do try to think of it as being a journey on a

cruise

A ride to the jaws of hell

In my own company, me the mystic damsel!

A scar you do hide, bleeding with light profuse

You never did realize that with it, you might

infuse

Yourself with even more darkness

So that you might even forget that you have been

blessed

A blessing needs no words of comfort

Though it does make love seen as an

abomination

For faced with it, cursed becomes the lover

Cursed with feelings of hatred filling your heart

for him, forever!

When life's harsh eyes did speak lies
Thunder did roll in from the skies
None could see your deep hunger
Except the one called humankind's bestower!

So learn to live with your blessing
Avoid unnecessary speculating
Love your own games
As if the rules were set by your own!

45. THE EARLY RISERS

Early risers do own the world
These words are always spoken in a loud hurl
Seen they are, by most of us, as being as pearls
Pearls wanting to be lauded with praises

Amidst everything, each one does see the
peacock's dance
Though it does hide itself behind a wall
The early risers, the mystics, do hear its call
How beautiful, they say, come let us join in this
dance

At nightfall, luminescent remains the moon's
crescent
Though the peacock does rest
Though the early risers turn into early sleepers
They still do make wonders

Who do weave dreams of the greatest kind
Who do build castles as magical as those in fairy
tales
Who except the early risers
Who except those who eyes are not blind to the
peacock's dance

Early risers do own the world
Little birds they are, hiding their true side, that
of being eagles
Prancing around all the times, they even turn the
tables easily
Why, they do even dance with the taste of
freedom on their souls!

46. DARK TIMES ARE ABOUT TO COME

I stared at a bottomless void
Letting my eyes turn here and there
My mind was soiled, lost was I in my own
anguish
I just remembered those words, cruel and filled
with venom

Nothing could stop the coming turn of events
Still, I do lament
Lost is my conscience
Lost in this world's abstract dance

Dark times are about to come, whispered the
Oracle
The evil witch does still reign with her broken
tentacle
Those darkened hours shall be my fort
For, in them, I shall try to find the lost light

While I did stare in an endless void
I dreamt of having a glimpse at the face of the
Lord
I dreamt of the holy dance
It shall indeed bind the dark times with
obeisance!

Blank and forlorn
My face was dull and thus I did mourn
I wished to see beauty
Beauty laden with purity

Is it too much to ask
Should I help myself in this task
For that, I certainly need to stop staring into the
void
I certainly need to start tending to the pains of
this world!

47. A GOD CREATED ENTITY

Can a God created entity lament
To such an extent
That even her life becomes adamant
Faced with her own whims, so recurrent?

Can a God created entity be in negativity
To the extent of creating animosity
Among those who share her own cosmos
Those who are in need of her magical ethos

Would you dare to believe
That she is indeed ready to grieve
At this sight of frugality
Known to be the most inconsistent reality

Life, harsh and cruel
Are you the hidden hell?
Hidden you are always behind the bluish veil
Trying to sound neutral when faced with the
entity's wail

If you are not so
Why then does the God created entity be in
sorrow
Pray, do show on her some mercy
So that her soul do be happy

Else, God will surely be angered
After all, with frugality, He wishes not to be
bothered
So let us all hope that the God created entity
Be at last, filled with peace!

48. SEARCHING FOR THE LORD

Memories in my head do flash
Filled they are with smoky ash
Imbibed with a past essence
The only fragrance having the power to make me
dance

Gone is that specter
The one I search for in each of my prayer
Illuminated are my pearly tears
Even gone, his lamps shall glow in my heart
forever

May the Holy Lord shower on me some blessings
May these give rise to many awakenings
Always are they uplifting and enlightening
Always are they thrilling and surprising

Memories do flash, giving vent to an eternal ode
to the Lord
Hidden He may be among the many horde
Yet, know that He alone is my gardener
The only one keeper of my garden, for forever!

Only for His grace I do seek
Even if, faced with the unreal, I do seem weak
Pray, loving is His gaze
So much that without Him, pale and lifeless do
seem to be my skies!

49. SILVERY MYSTERIOUS MOON

Silvery hue of the mysterious moon

Do you enjoy having been given such a boon

You easily do make us all swoon

We do feel the love and the glee even at noon

When inexistent and invisible thou art

You do give lovers and dreamers a new start

You do cure those fits and tantrums

You even make us all hear the beat of unseen
drums

At night, lovers do dance while being basked in
thy light

And dreamers do dream while being lost in thy
sight

Silvery hue of the mysterious moon

Do you have even a fateful name?

You do have the power to release our passion

You do ease our stress

Always full of care, always full of attention

Faced with you, love knows not any power

Nor does it know any other trivial matter

Except that of being basked in thy silvery hue

O darling, darling moon

Somehow I wish I could fly to you, and

dance on one of your dunes!

50.CRAVING FOR FREEDOM

Great expectations

Void visions

Reason shall not be in for this season

Unless love does fly in its unison

Gone indeed is the past

Happy days do never last

Gone with them, are those smiles, now turned

cold

Hearts have thus been given in pain, to the most

holy Lord!

Love seen now as something bitter

Love can only be made to hate the other

For hatred is somehow better

That way, the heart can now be kept safe!

Dull realm, a trip here makes me feel like I do
live in martyrdom
All the while, I do crave to fly in all wisdom
I do crave for freedom
Why, I am sure, someday it shall all be given, at
the time of liberation!

51. THE SEASON OF PURITY

The season of purity

It shall come, with the burst of creativity

Laughing we shall be, along with the rest of

humanity

Why at last, the lamenting monk shall be in all

serenity

The rains of sincerity

They shall come, washing down all of hypocrisy

Joyous shall be that season

Yes, innocence shall shine with good reason

O Gods of the Blessed Abode

See the world's pain through my ode

Love, love the child in me, she does wish for

solace

She wishes to see the supreme, only such can

win her embrace

When it shall come that season

So holy; scared shall be the great demon

He did bring us all to a state of abandon

For his sins, we have shown so much of

adoration

The season of purity

Could be well accompanied by servility

Fragile is the current time

But we shall wait, with patience and might!

52. THE MERCIFUL BANDIT'S LAIR

To feel impartial love showered with care
Why such can only be seen in the bandit's lair
The same one, known to be a queen, the one
with the magical hair
Living there, in her hidden lair, there where only
love does bloom
As if announcing the end of the doom!

Few are those lucky ones
Happy they seem to be, as happy as the golden
swans
Happy, lovely and homely
Thankful to have a seat secured next to the
queen's
A queen dearly cherished by the most holy Lord

A gift it is, bestowed on a lucky few

They reside there, close to the queen, waiting for

a cue

Honoring the Gods they shall be

Revering them as the only Lords of eternity

Why the queen shall be pleased, surely

Impartial love is indeed showered on those

stricken despair

Only the Lord can be the fallen ones' peer

Only the queen does cure the burden

Only in her lair does she give love

Why surely it is the heaven that I do mean!

How to reach that lair, do you wonder

Well, it is a place for those who revel not in their

own blunder

For those who care not for the unreal

For those who seek for it

With a heart filled only with wise wit!

53. LOVE AND ITS FALSE GLORY

Should you glance at his eyes, you would see
power
Why, he did take me up above this world,
someplace higher
Higher than the clouds, higher than the Lord's
abode
Someplace where only his eyes do shine, bright
and proud

Should you glance inside his heart, you would
see muck
To his ego, to himself he is still stuck
Only his voice counts
Only his will matters

Should you ask for a piece of his heart
Why you would end up all broken
Tested you shall be, tested for your standards
Tested for your birth, tested as if he was to give
you awards

Should you give to him your heart
Why, he shall see whether golden are your
feathers
Whether your shadow is wrinkled
Or whether you do answer to the title of Princess

Now, surely you do wonder about who I do mean
Worry not, his name matters not
Time did heal
Turning has been the life's wheel

But my heart does still feel
At times, it does make me ill
No, no, to love and its frugality I shall not give
myself
Not anymore, not a second more

Now I only choose to see life's best
Surely, surely it is all a test
A world we do live in, being as unreal as the
sighting of a ghost
A world in which I am neither a guest nor a host

So, make the glory of Love, love all of creation,
Love, like me, without any reason
But never oh never give your heart to anyone in
particular
It shall make of you, none else other than a
miserable beggar!

54. THE LORD'S WATCHFUL EYES

Heavy was the penalty

Harsh words were written in the treaty

Peace has already been lost and bliss has been

shattered

For the downtrodden, nothing mattered

Gone were those seers of mysticism

They did crave to be lost in the holy prism

Yet, nothing did give them solace

They only waited for an embrace, a kind of a

genuine grace

Now, bright days were meant for torment

None could elude the detriment

For though happiness was well meant

Everyone still craved for the spiritual, to be its

mendicant

Seeing the chaos, from up the clouds, watching
the loss, was the Lord
Stern were his eyes, through them he could
never speak of any lies
He did attract the beautiful butterflies
His abode was what strived to attain the wise!

Yet, no more are seen those men so wise
Such is the reason why heavy was the penalty
Now everyone does wait for the second coming
Surely it shall be really uplifting!

55. MERCY TO EACH

Courage be to the downtrodden
Someday no more shall they be fallen
Peace shall help them rise with light
Serene, their demons shall cease to fight

Love be to those evil pirates
With hatred, they keep at those gates
There, where keepers become losers
And lovers turn into warriors

Mercy be to the mistaken witches
With pain, they stick to their stitches
Labelled, their pure heart becomes tarnished
And with time, love becomes all blemished!

Respect be to the martyrs

Shame faced they are, for they are here, mere

satires

Graced, they shall someday be applauded

When the Heavens with their presence shall be

loaded

Mercy, mercy be to my self

May my verses reach the most Holy Self

The one to fill with divine essence

This great illusory world of magnificence!

56. A TALE OF LOVE

While she did fly on her broom over the dark
towers
The enchantress did lose all of her mystical
powers
A merciful seer did fall for her
He did steal her powers, for, so seductive was her
flutter!

Kidnapped she was, captured and locked in his
dungeon
Scared, she cried as if she was a slave in hell
She realized not that love knows nothing except
selfishness
For the holy seer displayed nothing except
amorousness

Loving was the seer, pining for his new peer

Alluring was the maiden, always was she beauty

laden

His feelings were genuinely sincere

He saw his new days as being completely love-

stricken

She remained cold though

She desired her freedom

Basking always as the solo enchantress

Lost in her magic, her own mystic

But after the dawning of a new moon

She smiled, and the seer thanked the sky for

that boon

She became tender and loved him hereafter

So that she became his dear companion, full of

wonder

She did seduce him

She hid behind her smiles, her own intent

She wanted to regain her lost powers

She wanted to fly once more, over the towers

And on a dark stormy night
When lightning struck bright
In a wonder movement, she struck her wand
And got her powers back in hand

She was about to leave, jubilating, for her palace
When she cried, seeing her seer, her solace
Her heart bled and instead of leaving
She stayed back, for the want of a kiss

She did hold him close to her heart
She confessed of her evil act
That of wanting her own part
And with him she did make a loving pact

Overjoyed, overwhelmed, the seer let his tears
flow
Along with them, his feelings did fly high
With her side, his life would indeed be sweeter
Hence, together, their love held on, hereafter!

From that day on, love did get its name

Very well known today, a tale did make its fame

An enchantress and a holy seer

Forever to be with each other!

57. QUESTIONS AND ANSWERS

What is thy name

Asked to me my own shadow

I am only a flame

A flame, frail, scared of any imminent tomorrow!

What is thy essence

Asked to me my conscience

I am part of my own existence

Part of creation's dance

Where is thy heart

Asked my lonely solo part

Lost it is, since the decade's start

I gave it to the Holy Lord as a most holy gift!

Why dost thou pine then

Asked to me my Beloved, forever to be mine

I am that evergreen line

That which keeps you and the rest of the world,

happy and fine!

Where are you then, O Beloved

I asked him searching for his presence

Where are you, I see you not around

I am here, subtle and gentle always as are all the

mysteries

Shall my name then be known someday

Or shall I be forever a mystery

Let it be such then, said the overjoyed Beloved

Let it be such while you do enjoy a mortal nature

58. MY TIRED HEART

My heart knows not any rest
Once, in his company it thrived best
Now, I can only pray, Hear me O Lords of Fate
My best life shall have to bear the imprint of
being his mate

Thought I my pain would subside with time
I was wrong, for it only does grow and grow
So much that memories
Keep me in a state of eternal worries

Pray life do allow me to breathe
Always am I in a state of grief
But if you do show me a new corner
Why I am sure I will be better

Someday you shall end
Someday, I shall come to seek your truth
For now, do give me what I need
Do give me what I do need as to what I deserve

My heart knows not any rest
Though in his company it thrived best
It seeks new ways
Filled with both sunny and rainy days

59. A HUMBLE HEART OR AN ARROGANT MIND

Could you just close your eyes,
Close them, please do
Let yourself rise up, high up in the skies
Let yourself see this world, from high up, see you
the maze, the zoo

See you the lost purity
The forgotten Humility
See you the stunning stupidity
See you why, to everything here, I do laugh, I do
laugh and shake my head

I am pretty sure, when God made the Man
He did tell him, I am sure, He did say, Humble
shall be thy heart
But such has already been forgotten, Man to
himself does now tend
He has forgotten that to Humility he has to be a
support

Now in today's days, the Mind did take over
See you how it is filled with more than one
blunder
Arrogance does make it jubilant
Arrogance does make it even flippant

A humble person nowadays does seem weak
To him, each and everyone would simply smirk
An arrogant person does seem to show power,
He will evoke fear, and respect, why faced with
him, everyone shall cower

A humble person is for me, a piece of beauty
A pearl of the purest kind
While an arrogant one is simply a trumpet
Being blown today, why it shall be out of tune as
soon as it does get outdated!

Pray, be not so wild

Love and do be mild

Love and do be kind

I am sure, from such you shall benefit in the

end!

60. THE LOSS OF REASON

When reason does give way to insanity
Life takes it all with cruelty
For the stricken ones, it does show not any pity
For the stricken ones, it does give not any
serenity

Bearing with the wills of the demons
That of always neglecting sermons
The stricken ones can only wait
The hour it seems, is running late

Placed they are, on a chosen path
There where they can only laugh
For they have been chosen
After all, they are those who have a heart of
stone!

Life in such a beautiful world, is but illusory
It does paint a beautiful picture of creativity
Such, though does get shown as mere absurdity
For life does end abruptly

So when reason does give way to insanity
Why, one should wonder about its essence
What seems unreal here can be real in another
realm
Those who seem stricken here can be those who
do rule in another realm!

61. A REASON SIMPLY

The essence of life
I do keep wondering about
Is it all about faith
Is it a mere wait for death

The essence of death
Such brings to me great joy
New ways opening up to my soul
New avenues bringing me closer to the Lord

The call of my heart
Such do I discard with mere casualness
Of what use is the meaning of love
If not only to be lust in disguise

And what of the aim of living

Such has brought about great philosophizing

In what to believe

In having an aim or simply to be an accident of

science

The reason to be happy

Whether one be in great euphoria or in misery

Is surely the test of the Lord

To see whether someday we do deserve a reward

And what would I make of myself

After all this pondering

Pray, if you do have an answer

Lend it to me, so I may say faithfully my daily

prayer!

62. SUMMER MOON

Sweet and delicious, that's how I see the moon
on this summer night
Unlucky is indeed the one who is deprived of
such a sight
Moon of love, moon of Aphrodite
Moon of passion, moon of exaltation
Easy and peaceful I feel while being lost in its
contemplation
Reveries burst out in my heart, giving birth to a
lonely orgasm!

My heart is yet unattached, though still broken,
it pines to breathe with love
O summer moon, how beautiful you look, as if
you are made of eroticism
O creation of the wondrous kind, I wish you
could give me a sign of the world above
Near your charm, I wish to waltz with love, either
of an earthly kind, or filled with mysticism!

Placed 6th in the Contest
Poem of the week
Contest on Poetrysoup.com
Judged on 8/23/2014

63. UPON A BED OF PETALS

Upon a bed of petals

We became like Gods in murals

There, we burnt all our passion

By letting go of all our negation

Upon a bed of petals

I heard the Angels' recitals

When love bells are rung

When love songs are sung

Upon a bed of petals

I saw opening all those portals

Leading to the solace of your arms

Melting I became faced with the wrath of your

charms

Upon a bed of petals

We bid life to show us the boreals

Given to us by a grace of the Lord

When He was merciful enough to give us his

word

Upon a bed of petals

I became lost in depths, abysmals

There, in your eyes,

Was the expanse of the skies

64. TO THE HEART OF MY ISLAND

An ode to this busy city
My favourite in all of my country
Called Port Louis
Seen as the haven of bliss

Merchants, shops, offices, quays
Comes to mind the image of soldiers in khakis
A city sometimes brandishing celebrations
Some other times witness to great destructions

Joyful it is most of the times
Sorrowful at some other times
O city of my dreams, always so bountiful
Thou art the heart of this island, so beautiful!

Pray do gather yourself, get up, awake
Our people need your strength for our own sake!

65. HUSBANDS ARE IN HEAVEN
WHOSE WIVES SCOLD NOT

So much emphasis is placed today on the role of
the wife
She is to be pure, pristine, just, hardworking
She is to imbibe all who surround her with faith
She needs to be able to know everything without
ever asking

She is to be the woman behind her husband
The one who would make of him a gem
To be a wife, is surely a complicated state
Acted out badly, one can even be a contraband!

But what of the duties of a man,
Is he as important as the woman
To be a husband requires one only to work and
bring money
To care not whether the home is, without him, in
harmony

Husbands are in heaven whose wives scold not
Husbands have rights, rights to use words of
spite
Rights to beat, rights to abuse
Rights even to cheat, to hurt and bruise

When the woman speaks out, or scolds such a
man
She becomes something seen by some as a
legend
Seen by others as un-womanly
Whatever, she knows how to protect herself
through her duty

What of those men whose wives scold not
Should they be brought back to the pot
To be cooked and simmered
To be brought to the right path

Feminists, equal rights, equal opportunities
Women's places no more being in the kitchen
Husbands, change your mentalities
We, women, we are frail and easily broken!

Placed 10th in the Contest :Husbands are in

heaven whose wives scold not

Poetrysoup.com

Contest Judged on 1/3/2014

66. WOMAN, THE EPITOME OF FRAGILITY

Woman, different from Man
Yet, considered by some as alien
Why, some of you may ask?
She knows her established task
Still, she fights for her right!

Blessed by the Gods, with a gift
That of rescuing those adrift
She gives life, she gives solace
In return, she has to know her place
Woman, you are needed though unheeded!

Those known as the stronger
Shamelessly wrong Her, known as the weaker
Raped, duped, cheated, beaten
Even if only at Her feet, they see Heaven!
Those, who see in the woman an object!

Careful! Caution! Think of the consequence
Each action of Hers should be done in adherence
The eyes of the city is always ready
To judge and blame her that Lady!
Whether it is Pregnancy or Infidelity!

Woman, called Feminine or Emancipated
Her fragility remains accentuated!
Luck and Fate play their game on her hand
Abused or placed on a pedestal in the Man's
Land
She remains the one with the hidden Force!

67. LETTER FROM MY MUSE

Smile, urged my muse
Smile as you do fondly muse
Your chosen path may be full of thorns
Lush sometimes do appear the lawns
Yet, Evil does remain hidden in its soils

Smile urged my muse
While being in my shelter, you shall never lose
Do learn to face this hoary weather
Do face the howling wind blowing away thy sole
feather
After all, I am here to suit the needs of your own
temper

Remember that blessed you are by the Most
Revered Lord
Do spread His light, His word
Should you need some help
Just think of me and you shall feel me
After all I am but your loving muse

So said, I grabbed pen, so whimsical
And wrote my verses, so lyrical
In ode to my muse,
To my friend, the one healer of my every bruise
Given to me by the insensitivity of Man!

68. TO BE

To miss a ghost
The one I love most
Makes life seem to be a frightening journey
To live in emptiness
Yearning always as would the lonely Goddess
Yearning for a sign of tenderness,
Remains my own sad Fate

To cry out in agony
For that chosen Fate, chosen impulsively
Yet, even with faith placed on the Lord, so Holy
Gives life an aspect so lovely!
To long for a glimpse
For that which can make my heart wince
For that which when deprived I am,
Makes me choose to pray for my death
Reminds me of love's great depth!

Shall it someday shine
My luck, my Fate
Shall it someday cease, that pain
Never did I choose for that on my own
Rather, it was given to me as a boon

Life is but a journey, true
We do wish to, yet, we can never run from it
Fallen we certainly are here in this world
Still, we can dare to dream to rise up once again.

69. ALL THAT I AM

Power does mystify me
Power emanating from the skies
Power, from the unknown
The only thing which allows me to be

Love does attract me
Love from the other realm
Love of another kind
Love, of such a kind, as willing me to leave
everything else behind

Life does put me into desolation
A harsh and hard one it is
Here, one is indeed meant to toil
To suffer and to enjoy false pleasures

God does bewilder me

If He does be

Why, O Why, did He have me fallen, sick on

Earth

If He does be, why does He not make Himself felt

and seen?

Being delved deep in an art, does allow me to be

free

In it, I feel that I am being myself

A poet is all I am

A poet of the mystical, a poet seeking to find the

real!

70. RELIEF

It pricked me as if it were the rough caresses
from His hand
Those, given to me as a boon for my own stand
A stand always so scary and so mysterious
A stand being always like a maze for the curious
Those who are lost in a moment in time
When disease and unrest soar up high at their
prime

It warmed me up as if it was the golden gaze
from His eyes
It certainly does not seem to be the proper
convention for the wise
Bad tempered could become the skies
If I do voice out what it is that I speak of
After all, belief and faith are meant not to be
shaken
The Holy Books do speak words of Truth

Yet, the Lord's wish shall shine with all
magnificence
My life is always imbibed with His essence
My Fate I do leave to Him, I do surrender to Him
Whether He brings me to His own ends
Whether He leaves me yearning for it
For that which pricks me and warms me, for that
which I seek!

71. MY PRAYER

Love me with loads of grace
I begged, seeking to find in love some solace
Leave me not in disgrace
Let me be the Lord's own sweet dove
Let me bask in His comfort
Filling me up with sweet kisses
Shining on us all, many a bliss
May the Lord Bless
His darling creatures lost in their adventures!

Take me to the highways
There where flowers do linger on the alleys
May they appear beauteous for the courteous
So much that gems shall no longer seem
precious
Divine songs would no more be at a loss
Life itself would seem glorious
And demons shall be slain, oblivious
Though they do appear gracious

They do disrupt that which is always so
harmonious!

Pray do love me with grace
Such was my prayer, when I looked at the skies
After all, life is but a fall
A fall down an invisible wall
Someday, we shall move
Someday, we shall see
Someday, we shall be loved
Meanwhile, I care to see only the real
That which is not seen or felt in the world of the
temporal!

72. OF WHAT USE

Of what use is regret

If with hatred, it is all set?

Of what use is longing

If no more, is love to be singing?

Misunderstandings, cruel words

All stronger than my own swords

When Time did reach its climax

My verses could not show the meaning of their

own syntax

Yet, of what use is regret

If with dark designs it is bent

Cherished shall be always the past

Even if with thorns its setting is now cast

Best it is to learn to love the present

Best indeed to pretend that we are all free

Happy, no more in torment

No more searching for the past, or worrying

about the future!

73.   THE MAGIC OF MY PEN

A magical pen in my pocket
My dairy tucked in my jacket
I ran, with my twinkling amulet
Away to the refuge, offered by the warmth of the
cabaret

Sitting by the corner, lost in a swirl
I dream of that brave new world
Panacea-ic, lovely, peaceful
No more devilish and sinful

My magical pen does begin to work, guided by
my muse
Words flow in verses, with faith in profuse
Those words, meant for the High Lord
A message of love from the one among his horde

Craving to fly with Him
Yearning for Him, dazed as if in a dream
I write, while the dancers excel
And the demons cry in hell

The moment after, a magic carpet appeared
Taking a seat, on it I flew high
Above the clouds, there where He is much feared
There where the road to happiness hears not the
question why

Riding on the carpet, flying as an angel
I soared high and sang a duet
There, in the land that I dream of
The land of peace and love

As I did open my eyes
I saw that I was but lost in a dream of my own
A dream of the wondrous kind
A dream as being the only one of its kind

What a marvelous dream it was

To dream while being fully conscious

To experience the real while being lost in the

unreal

Indeed, everyday, I shall attempt to be in the

cabaret!

74. FOLLOWING HER OWN COURSE

When she killed the bandit
The Queen was seen as the rogue one
Gorgeous though she was, even seeming pure
So much that her murderous act got her lost in
absurdity

Remembered as the Beauteous One
She was now revered as the Rebellious One
Lonely, yet, surrounded she was by her acolytes
Dreaming of a rescue which could take her to
great heights

None do wish to be blessed with her sight
Angered, the Queen easily did put up a fight
She killed again, for no reason
And became accused of treason

Sent into an unwanted exile

She did fume and seethe for a while

For even if he did like her smile

The King cared not to see her again

Bleeding, wailing and yearning was her heart

None could see through her pain

All could see a mere wall

Rebelling against laws, wishing to be in stall

She lived on with faith and pain

To herself, her life did seem to flow in vain

She waited, though, for a rescue, like an eternal

monument

A cure, to ease all of her ailments!

75. THE POWER OF LOVE

A lonely mistress
Was sent into great distress
She was told she was heartless
And for her distress found no other cure other
than being breathless

Pain gripped her soul
None would listen to her call
None could even hear her cries
And so the lonely mistress turned a deaf ear to
the world

She did not want to seem grim
With tears sparkling on her face
She did not want to seem frail
By telling the world that her heart had been
broken into a thousand pieces

So she chose to ask for deliverance
She would be free from the life of eternity
She would live on Earth
As a maiden of simplicity

But the Lord missed her
So much that he came after her
As a being of great worth
He did save her from her chosen tomb!

Once more, she was taken up the skies
Once more she was made the Queen
For love is stronger than everything
Love can even stretch across the many barriers!

76. TALE OF A PRINCE AND LOVE

When love got transformed into vapor
Life lost its eternal color
It did fade faced with the dark illumined ardor
Of the evil prince, full of stolen valor!

A fair prince he was, of good breeding
Till he resorted to stealing
Then, nothing could prevent him from smiling
Specially not an evil act, so dehumanizing!

But still, love did knock on his doors
T'was on the day he chopped off the lions' paws
She was a weak maiden, so fair
So fair that none could claim to want to be her
pair

When their eyes did meet
They became lovers instantly
The maiden craved for his gaze
The way flowers craved for rain from the skies

Of marriageable age, they were to each other
betrothed
When O miracle, the prince into purity did soar
For the maiden did give him stars
Her lovely eyes were full of goodness

Love thus changed once more into radiance
Life did get back its colorful essence
Proud were the subjects
For the prince was no more evil, he now shined!

77. MY SECRET HOLY HIDEOUT

I do keep dreaming of that Holy Place
There where I shall find some grace
There, it is found, there, on the hidden
mountains
There, where nothing does get there, not even the
magical trains!

I do keep dreaming of love shining with
incandescence
Of genies dancing lost in their own trance
Of the unreal, of the magical
Of all that may seem wild

Far goes my young mind
Far into the unknown, into the dark
It goes there, even in the city basking in sin
Where go those who have been rejected!

That holy secret place is indeed my solace
The high Lord could only be there with His mace
Gentle He shall be, flowery shall I be
Lovely shall be the whole scenery!

In my dreams, I do keep shining in the Holy
Light
I am there at the feet of the Great One
My anguish does get ceased
Calm I am at last, for here, I shall live for ever!

78. THE FALSE WORDS OF THE ORACLE

Once, the fairy queen sought out the help of the
oracle
She asked, should I set my cards on the table?
Should I lay on my faith, love in ample?
What would be the meaning of my life
If while treasuring it, I do end it up while battling
with strife?

Queer, thought the oracle, with a smile
What could have happened to the Queen since a
while
Since she did meet the king of her life
She is always in deep worry
Poor queen, I shall make my predictions without
any ruse!

Gone shall be your woes, whispered the honest
mouth
Gone shall also be the evil wind, gone to the
south
Shouted the oracle, as would a child witnessing
a miracle
Hearing which, light became the queen fairy
Light, believing in the coming of her own story!

Yet, wrong was the prediction
Who could know about the ways of an unruly
king
The rogue, the brute, he dared to dupe
A young maiden, who was as innocent as a rose
On a calm night, he robbed her of her purity and
left her to herself

When the news reached the queen
Accursed she felt, accursed she became
No more did she believe in the words of the
oracle
She left the kingdom, she left it for another world
Hoping someday, she would find in a knight, the
purity that she seeks!

79. THE QUEEN OF ALL REALMS

Long live the Queen of all Realms
Lovely she is, even if she lives on alms
Long live the great Queen
The idol of each and everyone in all the worlds!

Gone may be her golden feathers
No more does she attend any suppers
Ready she is to face with any dangers
Hiding always in her satchel, all her daggers!

Assembled she is always with her guides
There where the sky opens wide
None dare to cause her anger
Everyone knows about her quick temper

Specially the king

Being evil in kind, he did leave her ailing

Being evil in kind, he did leave her suffering

Now, she does live on alms, yet, she does dream

of re-bonding

Yet, faithful she remains to her king

She did not hesitate to fight by his side

When the forces of darkness did strike

Yet, even after her victory, she did choose to go

back to living on alms

80. FOR THE ALL POWERFUL ONE

I sat, all alone in my fortress
I sought for a ready solace
I shall even be your temptress
For that bout of love, I shall even be selfless

The mysterious one he is, always full of charm
With eyes so sweet and warm
With an amount of indestructible beauty
Always basking in a calming serenity
Why, do I ask myself, how to make some sense
out of this love?

Through holy words, Through holy books
You try to bestow on the world, some bouts of
holy looks
My Lord, the all powerful one
Ruler of the three worlds, as the merciful one
Please do see me as your lover, always the pining
one!

O great Lord, a sanctuary is thy abode

For you is this eternal ode

Your name shall always be kept in my heart, as

my own secret

Lost in your thoughts, I do always laugh

For you, I shall bear with everything, even with

life's cough

Alone in my own company

I yearn for when I shall be in your garden

Happy in my solitude

I dream of your gracious comfort

Pray, Lord of Death, when shall this temporary

life end?

81. DUST FROM THE PAST

Like me, you surely know about the history of
our island
You surely know of the time when it was being
colonized
When it was still a dark and green forest
With dodos making everywhere their careless
nests

If like me, you are also a dreamer, then
Do let yourself rise
Like me do imagine the time of long ago
When the western world was just beginning to
land here

Imagine the beauty then, the freshness of the
island
Trees, dark and deep, ebonies
Rivers, seas, birds of all kinds
Plantations everywhere, animals of the most
gentle kind

I am sure, then, the time was right for love
Maidens dressed in lovely dresses
Would waltz at the hands of handsome charmers
Whether under the gleam of the silver moon, or
on the crystal clear beach

Imagine kisses shared and stolen
Imagine love as yet being forbidden
Imagine the beauty of the surroundings
The lovely parties done on the cool nights

Imagine the toils the first people had to go
through
When they did start to build everything
When they did choose to place the foundation
stone
When they did fight off the first horrible cyclone

Maybe I was here living as a fresh maiden

Newly snatched from my homeland

Having been brought to the land of burden

Meeting then, here, the love of my life

Making then of my island, the worldly paradise

Making here, like the dodos, my nest, my prize

Well of all this I can only allow myself to dream

A dream of love it is, in a most ancient setting!

Placed 6th in the Contest Pick a Title

Contest sponsored on Poetrysoup.com

13/11/2014

82. THE SECRET OF THE PYRAMIDS

If I could bring to my life some changes
I would choose to have another birth
A birth occurring not in our era
A birth occurring rather, at the time of
Cleopatra's rule
Mystified I am by that epoch
An epoch of unsolved puzzles surely
How could Man build such monuments?
When He himself was just a toddler
Learning about all that does surround Him
Learning about all that does make Him be

Why, surely I would come to see those who built
mazes
Why, surely I would come to know about why
were the dead mummified
Does life surely continue after death
Does life end here with the body just turning into
dust
If I was an Egyptian priestess, I would have been
able to decipher it all

Whereas now I am still, spent and worn
I do read of ancient Egypt
And I am lost in my own enthrall
I can only dare to dream
Life is itself but a dream
If not, why would yesterday be rubbed off
Rubbed off from our minds
From our actions
Why would it remain only as a memory
And why would we hope
Hope about having a better future
When it is but a frugality
Life does end,
Life does not mend!

Did Man take eons to build pyramids

Or was Man then, some sort of superman?

Pray, for knowledge I do thirst

If I could change anything about my life

I would choose to have a new birth

A birth in the ancient city of Egypt

Would I live then by the side of those,

Those who were close to the secrets of the skies!

83. FORCED LOVE

Strange are the happenings on this lovely
evening
Strange indeed with the coming of the great
Viking

He came especially for the lonely maiden, alone
always in her garden
With joy and feelings of love she was always
smitten

Finally, her garden she chose to leave, quite a
surprise
For the maiden, other than her garden, remains
always in her dark towers

Graced she shall be with the Viking's coming
A dark prince he was, with a smile oh, always so
charming

Love struck he has been ever since he was
around her
Always with a gleeful heart which he wishes to
astound

Confused he was as well
He hopes to have her love, else, he shall have to
use a love spell

He was indeed with a mixed state
Tonight, the maiden's answer shall be his own
fate

No one knows of her inner self
Her heart, she has it kept on a shelf

Exchanged with the Lord, for a dull piece of
stone
For once, to fragility, she had been too easily
prone

When Time did come for the world to know of her
agreement
None could see her hidden inner torment

He, pining and striving to be wedded
Her, wanting to have her ghosts buried and dead

Fortune played her own part
Surely, they do both deserve a new start

The ways of the days imposed on the prince to
have her kidnapped
He trusted it was the only way to have her blank
wall snapped

Wise indeed was this decision
For the maiden loved being in a love prison

A short moment of love being forced
Caused love to sparkle like gems, so happy and
rejoiced

No more did she remain as walled
Now, to love and joy she was propelled

Smile shined on her face

She was now, the prince's sole ace!

84. ON THIS WINTER'S NIGHT

The blistering cold stung from everywhere
Frozen was the flowing air

None could bask in joy and delight
No warmth could be felt specially not on this
night

When shall you leave, o cold winter
Waiting we all are for the summer

Brown are those leaves, stuck on the trees
Dead are the flowers, blooming not at their ease

Shiny are those twinkling drops of dew
Feeling as cold as ice the moment that night flew

No longer can birds be seen playing
No more can love be felt, not even in mourning

A mere glance, soothing, from two prying eyes
Searching, inquisitive, asking even, youth shall
you not be wise?

Barriers of age, barriers of law
Neither shall bells chime, nor shall hearts soar

Lingering only shall be the cold air
Filled with hatred, flying here and there

Accompanied with loneliness and barrenness
Empty I do feel in this abysmal coldness

85. MY SHORTCOMINGS

Being made of fragile sensibility
I relish being lost in my own creativity
Why, I even relish sharing it with the world
Such does make me feel like I am a special girl

But I am in all also made of shortcomings
They do take me to more than causing some
disturbing
I do interact with difficulty
With those who do make up the walls of my city

I prefer to be alone
To my own demons I do become prone
I do keep my judgments to myself
And do pretend to be a solo queen, seated on the
highest shelf

But hey, I do have a conscience

Many a times, it does show its magnificence

I do feel guilty, if I have been too cruel

I do show humanity, to those caught in my spell

I do have a sense of duty as well

Even if all I do wish is to be a rebel

A rebellious dreamer

Safe under her own cover

I do care to do my duty

With all sense of civility

So in the end I guess it all makes me a good

person

One who can be trusted, for whatever reason!

Placed 1st in the contest, My shortcomings

Poetrysoup.com

9/11/2014

86. WHILE BEING IN SIN CITY

The day wore on noisily
Even bird's songs were drowned recklessly
None could dream of happiness
Their minds were teeming with stress

Anxiety, Impiety, Cruelty
All flew around in sin city
None could care about poetry
None, not even those basking in spirituality

The day wore on, till came dusk
The Lord's favorite smelled of musk
Immersed with the divine nectar
She dreamt of love

She dreamt of love, there, where purity reigns
There, where they do sit, the sovereigns
Full of life they are, yet full of disdain
For tainted is the illusory veil, tainted with evil

Temporary is this reality

Even so, none can be beyond its glasses

Except for her, the seeker of peace, the favorite of

the Lord

Graceful, fragile, she chose not to remain blinded

As beautiful as the show of artifice

She craved for only one edifice

That of her Lord being so glorious

That of being held on a quest, so pious!

The day wore on noisily

How dumb does seem to be all of humanity

Relying only on whatever is sensory

Discarding all that could be of a real nature!

87. LOVE

Love is indeed something so precious
Of all the gems, its seeds are yet so dangerous
It does cause the fall of the pretentious
While ending up with the one always so gracious

Love is indeed a boon, the most merciful
Forgiveness and hope binds it down, it does
seem so beautiful
In the end, the result becomes so bountiful
For when it is graced with mercy, living does
become so cheerful!

Love is meant to be tested
Such has been, by the beloved, resiliently
attested
To be loved at all costs, even in stubbornness
Does make both the lover and the beloved bear
with each other

Love is one of the most potent blessings
Yes, does keep it flowing in thy daily livings
With it, each day and each night does be so
pleasing
Even if the rain comes between each shining!

Love is a gift, the one sweetest
With time, it shall be seen as the brightest
Peace, serenity, all do rest with the beloved
As without Him, everything else does seem
withered!

88. A SAD TALE OF LOVE

Sad is the mystic, one who always was so
agnostic
No more did he crave to find creation's relic
For abandoned he is by the Queen
So lost he was in himself, while being all mean!

A seer he is, one devoid of any emotions
Relinquishing only in whatever be called the
divinity
Never did he realize that his Queen was in
neglect
So concentrated he was in his own intellect!

Such caused her heart to pain, she was horribly
hurt
The ways of the one she called 'My King' could
not be so curt
Lamenting, she ran to hide in the forest
Singing odes to her lost love, to her painful
stance

Horribly bothered was the seer
Though he always did crave for only one peer
His God, His Lord, the one always with his sword
The one Ruler of the great Heavenly abode

Now, the absence of his Queen was unbearable
She had been, through all her whims, so
adorable
No more did he yearn for the nirvana
No more did he yearn for the eternal

Queer Queen, she hid, she cried, so much that
she became stony
She remained like that, in a hidden cave, waiting
to be saved
Time did go by, she turned into a statue
Why, her wait having been long overdue

The King did find her at last
Sorry, he was for he could not save her
He did crave for the past
When together, they made life seem happier

He sat and cried
Wishing he could change her back
But nothing could be done about it
So he swore to make the whole world bow to that
statue

He travelled through deserts, through the seas
He did have more than one follower
Blessed he was, for the whole of humanity chose
to pray to the Queen
Why, thought he, someday he shall meet her,
somewhere up above the clouds!

89. THE POWER OF THE HEART

The life story of the Queen

Is so painful that it need be written in red ink

So painful was her existence

Her fate having been chosen by her King, and no

one else!

A beautiful one she was

One as fair as the lilies

White as the purest snow flakes

Radiant, even more than the gleam of the sun

Never was she meant to be loved

Precious she was for the Lord

Jealous he became if she was approached

For every little thing, he had her reproached!

She remained faithful
She pretended she was blissful
So much that the world called her the
submissive one
So much that the world looked at her with envy

Knowing not that she was always in misery
Suffering and pining was her constant mood
A brooding queen, life was for her, real mean
Her King left her always to seek other pleasures

One day, she could take it no more
She fled, with a heart, so sore
She fled to a world, being so false
And its every disease, she did endorse

The King did find her missing
He cared not, for she was but an object
After all, he could have her replaced
She was, only one of the many who had a pretty
face

Then came a day when she prayed with devotion
Asking the Goddess of Mercy to be relieved of
this curse
Yes, life in the false world, could be but a curse
Asked she, to be made into nothingness, to have
her soul dissolved

The whole of the Heavens heard her
Repentant became her King
Only then did he see her frail essence
Only then did he cry out for a change of situation

Mercy shined in the false world
The Queen was lifted up to the heavens
She looked into the eyes of her king
And knew at once, that she would now, joyfully
wear his ring!

90. I AM

I am just matter
My skin made of flesh and blood
Life's own particle

I live everyday
A poet in misery
Seeking to find it

That which has been lost
That which can never be found
That which has no name

Know I what I seek
I would share it with you
Unknown it remains

Love I my own soul
Sure, for it is eternal
Though it is unseen

My life I do live
As it is meant to be lived
Following my fate

I am, obviously
I have a family name
I live, sure, I do

I do ask myself
Of the ways of this realm
Wait I for my death

Eager to see it
The gate of eternity
To be with the Lord

In the end, you ask
Do I really know myself
I would say, I don't!

91. THE ANGEL FAIRY

Could you just imagine, walking by a fairy
One filled with beauty
But one who is so angry
Angry at the turn of humanity

She came to earth for an unknown reason
Now, she feels like she is in a prison
She wished she could have her magic wand
So she would clear every nook of this land

She is indeed all powerful
One look at her and one just feels beautiful
She has pink fiery hair
And a strong steady stare

She walks around the globe
Wishing there was a way, the heavens she could
probe
She is dressed always in a sexy white robe
One which would make even the beauty queens
sob

She has on earth, no lover
After all, a fairy and a human being cannot be
together
She waits for her death, true
While wishing she could cure this world of its
blue

She is heartbroken, but nothing can mend her
She does have a frail and fragile temper
Why, what would you say to such a being
Should you meet her while walking?

Placed 6th in the contest Sketch a Character
Poetrysoup.com
3/11/2014

92. ANGER AND LOVE

Anger sparked an intent

When venom was added to it, it became a

torment

Lost felt those stricken souls, treading against

that current

Yet, anger did thrive on love

Anger did turn into love

Love for the downtrodden

Love sparkling new flowers in my garden

Anger turned it all into a blessing

To love and to be loved

Why, none could be luckier than me

None, except the one being always so charming!

Anger caused love to be bonded

Without it, existence would have been absconded

Of what use would have been my conscience

Should it not be, with love, eternally adorned!

A blessing in disguise

It did fill up the grey skies

Love and delight

Did shine brighter than the starlight!

93. THE LORD'S COMING

My heart flutters
My soul dances
My Lord is close
His absence has been the cause of my woes
Absent from my life since the day I took birth
I have been without Him, in a state to shed only
tears

Since the past days
I can only jump to life's sways
O hearty muse
Shower on me some pity, with passion in profuse
My Lord is much awaited
Without Him, cold and desolate has been my
heart
Now, I am sure it shall be filled with love in
ample

Always does He ride on His golden horse

There, I can feel Him, coming with passion in His

heart

Powerful, Omniscient, He is not the transient

A virtuous Queen

For Him, I remained pure

Never did I yearn for the obscure

Though with disgrace, I did wilt

Yet, the promise of eternal solace did give my

soul a new tilt

O heart, be patient!

O fate, be lenient!

O Lord, be loving!

Be loving, frail is my tender heartling!

Be loving and do tend to my yearning!

94. RESPECT FOR HUMANKIND

Pray, do you know what I do mean

When respectful I do wish you seen

Do you care for humanity

Do you care by showing respect

For all that does be imperfect

Do you have this humility

Pray, do you know what I do mean

When respectful I do wish you seen

Arrogance fills up every nook

Deviance follows it by hook

Do you care for humanity

Do you have this humility

Pray, do you know what I do mean

When respectful I do wish you seen

Placed 8th in the contest : Sonettina Rispetto

6/11/2014

Poetrysoup.com

95. AN EVIL WORLD

Should I be able to send a message to the time
controller
I would surely let him know of the danger
The seeds of evil have been spreading
It looks like, he is busy sleeping!
Else, he would have strived
To have those dark days archived
Evil would merely be a curiosity
A past meant to be but a falsity!

O Time Keeper, how shall I make you feel my
throbbing tempo?
Do you see the immensity of my inner magneto
A tiny dynamo, fragile and frail
Hidden behind a silvery veil
Had I been by your side
I would have quickened the ride
So that evil would have flown away to hide!

Maybe I should pray to the Powerful Lord

Maybe I should offer him sweetened curd

Forgotten he has of this world

Or closed are his eyes, as he is lost in his own
play

Where he is, there is, after all, only harmony

There, where he is, only peace does prevail

There, love knows not any ailing

Come, my Lord, would I urge, come and see the
state of this world!

Yet, in spite of all my efforts

The Lord and the Time Keeper remain absent

Time and events are indeed interrelated

Fixed is the path of Fate

Yes, I believe the Dark Age shall be defeated

Remain quiet and let evil think it is winning

Only when the Time is right

Shall the Lord spread his light!

96. THE STEADY PACE OF LOVE

Steady was the ongoing pace

Love thrives not in haste

For hardships have I kept myself braced

As life and love are certainly not meant to be a

waste

Steady; yes; steady was the beat of my heart

Never greedy, it let Fate do her part

Yes, Fate has to cure and remedy the blatant

past

Love, without Fate's hand, certainly does not last

Moody was the fluctuating temper

In love, the current does never cease to flow

Even if walls do make around it, steady barriers

None can be more concrete than Fate's sooth

sayers!

In steadiness comes the readiness
Only when one is calm, shall the Lord bless
Those who deserve to be loved
Else, forever shall they remain fallen and
damned!

O Time, do keep showing me thy steady line
Love, being a blessing, is much heeded
Love, being a need, is much needed
So pray, even if moody is my temper, do allow me
to be steady!

97. SHALL I ASK THUS TO MY MATE

Do you intend to hurt
Do you intend to hate
Or do you intend to love
Such shall I ask someday to my mate

Bother you to ponder about my state
Brooding and moody is it, as at date
Love does give pain, love does make one vain
Yet, it shall not stop me from being bent on my
aim

That of living and laughing out loud
That of shining in my songs' sincerity
That of enjoying this world's spirituality
By making as if The Great Lord does walk on it

Physical love, temporal love, is even considered
immoral
Why, it is even seen as being part of the material
So, shall I say to my mate, if you do intend to
hurt and hate
Let us both go on our separate ways

In this way, I shall be left in my own
contemplating bliss
While you shall seek all that you did miss
This world and its joys are of no pleasure to me
What I seek is purity and eternity!

98. A TWISTED DANCE

The Angry Queen danced on,
Oblivious to the heat and the cold
She closed her eyes and danced
Like a mad woman, so bold
Her anger was venomous, even enormous
Her King had dared call her amorous
So she danced, without a single dress on

Of what use is her love
If she was to be labelled
Of what use is being taken for a dove
If she was to be backpedalled

The king was so sorry, so he joined the dance
He kept on his face a smile and sought to be
forgiven
He danced, beside her, from beginning to end
Till the time came to love and forgive

He did grab the Queen in his arms

And kissed her as if he was a hero, full of charms

Nothing could match his joy

When the lady's anger turned all coy!

She was stern at first

Then for the touch of his hands she did yearn

So much that soon, the pleasures of love were

beating in their full essence!

99. THE WAYS OF LOVE

Love knows not any surrender
Self gratifying, it turns one into a learner
The Beloved being a teacher who can only fly
higher
While the Lover being a traveler, travelling to the
state of ecstasy!

Love shines not in any sort of blunder
Written always it is in the famous note
hereunder
That all is fair in love and war
As none can erase passion from want and desire!

Love can only sing in harmony with itself
To someone deprived of it, death does brag
proudly
To have killed silently and slowly
To have been that which makes one guilty

Love is as special as the mysterious
Basking in it, one does turn, to everything else,
oblivious!
Oblivious even to all the sins flying around
As when struck with love, no more does one
stand on solid ground!

Such, such are the ways of love
Strange indeed, stranger than life
True, none can equal its mystery
Except maybe the one to create creativity!

100. PURITY OR PASSION

Two paths lay in front of me
One was lit with the colors of purity
The other was strewn with the colors of passion
And I
Stood, still, forsaken
Looking at them
And wondering which one to choose!

The battle that waged in me was horrific
My heart conflicted with my soul
My desires clashed with my principles
My feminine yearnings longed to be satiated
But my conception of life simply tried to
suppress these!

I stood, looking at them both for a long time

Dawns arose

And dusks dozed off

Each at their respective time

While, I, stood, just like a marble statue

Wondering at which would be my wisest choice!

But when existence itself had had enough

It blew across my gaze

A stark picture of truth

Which, when I lay my eyes on, shook and jolted

me!

Pray, I knew then, which was to be my choice

Passion is bound to bring heartbreaks,

Purity, on the other hand, brings about sooth

and peace!

Placed 6th in the Contest MY EASTER PREMIUM
any theme any form max 25 lines
Contest Judged: 19/4/2017
Poetrysoup.com

AFTERWORD

I have known Anoucheka as a student of mine during her degree course and I can say that she already then showed signs of great ambition and determination.

I have been in touch with this budding poet in my capacity as Chairperson of the President's Fund for Creative Writing, as we have published her books and I can affirm that I am amazed by the work stamina displayed by this young lady.

As a writer myself, I can but congratulate this new generation writer for being such a prolific element in the world of Mauritian Literature.

In this new anthology entitled "A Poet's Secrets" Anoucheka has delivered verses to the best of her abilities, where she roams freely among the literary devices and technicalities with great verve and majestically. In her own words " I walk in a flowery garden, a dance in the courts of Eden"

Furthermore, she will add about her own existence and her identity, in this dream world where she is "The queen of my words" And she moves on regally showing mastery over the language used by being "the queen of all mystics".

I could discern great admiration she shows for British Poetry, specially as she relates her love for poetry with words of John Donne to write on the mysterious aspects of the mighty Sun and the more powerful entity called Death.

Anoucheka grows so fast in her poetry, despite her young age and philosophically points out that "What is Love, if not Lust in disguise" I can simply say I am amazed here, as I compare her with the vain young people of today and applaud her great maturity and wisdom

One may then question her prowess, her dexterity, her literary skills at such a young age. She gives the answer, she believes in the Almighty and her faith in God leads her to great heights. She writes "For my Lord, I remain always thirsty"

On this note, as a friend and as a fellow writer, I wish this queen of words greater faith in the supreme power governing our lives and warm feelings for a very bright and flourishing future in the magical world of Literature.

Dr[Mrs] Anitah Aujayeb

Chairperson, President's Fund for Creative Writing

Ministry of Arts and Culture

Mauritius

May 2017

AUTHOR'S BIO

Anoucheka Gangabissoon is a Primary School Educator in Mauritius. She writes poetry and short stories as hobby. She considers writing to be the meaning of her life as she has always been influenced by all the great writers and wishes to be, like them, immortalized in her words.

Her works can be read on poetrysoup.com and she had also appeared in various literary magazines like SETU, Different Truths, Dissident Voice, In Between Hangovers Press, WISH Press, Tuck's Magazine, Blue Mountain Review, among others. She has also been published in Duane's Poetree and also in two anthologies for the Immagine and Poesia group. Her poems are often placed in free online contests

Table of Contents

Thank you for taking the time to read ***A Poet's Secret***.

If you enjoyed it, please consider telling your friends or posting a short review. Word of mouth is an author's best friend and much appreciated.

Thank you, Anoucheka Gangabissoon.

www.ingramcontent.com/pod-product-compliance
Lightning Source LLC
Chambersburg PA
CBHW051417090426
42737CB00014B/2714